"Myth and modernity weave together in *On Distance*, Emily Ahmed's first collection of poems – it is a remarkable book of quiet insight; the beauty inside these poems is born from their purity and striking clarity, but purity is no place of piousness here and Ahmed approaches it with a reverence for ambivalence. An instability in language, location, and love cohere in the poems; the elusive search for home drives the speaker to probe language which offers no resolution – in this, we readers, receive a gift."

-Elisabeth Houston, author of *Standard American English*

"The memoir and the memorial, with all their 'dangerous tongues' building and destroying bridges, the Arab as American and the American as Arab: Emily Ahmed, a poet who aspires to 'age like a country', or like a Penelope, always between leaving and being left."

-Fady Joudah, author of *[...]*

"In *On Distance* Emily Ahmed writes about cities with blue eyelashes. Some of her poems capture the language of separation. They ask us to love in the old language. They remind us to remember family as one tries to rebuild the heart. There are lines that glitter in this collection. This book introduces an exciting new voice to our literary landscape."

-E. Ethelbert Miller
Writer and literary activist
2023 Grammy Award Finalist in the category of Spoken Word and Poetry

On Distance

On Distance

Poems

Emily Ahmed

ELYSSAR PRESS
Newport Coast, CA

Printed in the United States of America

First Printing, 2025
ISBN 979-8-9898850-2-2

Elyssar Press
3 Calvados,
Newport Coast, CA 92657

www.ElyssarPress.com

Cover illustration by Emily Ahmed
Cover and book design by Stephanie Aoun Bou Karam
All photographs by the author, and are used with appropriate permissions.
Images by rawpixel.com / freepik.com

For the outsiders

table of contents

On the airplane

I carry one book for each language,
one for my mother,
one for my father.
I do not have enough time to read both.
I do not have enough time to know both my mother and father.

على الطائرة

أحمل معي كتابا لكل لغة.
واحد لأمي،
واحد لأبي.
ليس عندي وقت كاف لأقرأ الكتابين.
ليس عندي وقت كاف لأعرف أمي وأبي.

Arrival

Possibility: a spell that wants to be uttered
in a language you don't quite remember. You
try to pluck words from your dreams, make
a list of phrases to translate:
To deserve
To drool
To forgive (oneself)
Pathetic
How to ask for directions
How to give directions
Intuition

So, wandering and welcomed, you find
there is an inn at the edge of the darkest forest,
a mirage in the brambles and vines that one day
solidifies. You'll have come a long way, your thighs
scratched and your boots grubby, embraced by a
film of dust that captures old memories. The innkeeper
will offer you her spare slippers, red and striped,
will tell you, *get used to people coming and going.*

Enter: here, the shy women are posing for the
cameras, the visionary girls running the show, their
braids as intricate as their minds. Here, how they curl
into themselves to become, not smaller, but closer on
the couch, to make room for all, *the movie is about to
start, sh, shhh.* Jello for dinner. After a month, you buy
a lamp for the first time since you were nine, when
you and your mother sat on cushions on the floor in an
empty flat for months before the furniture arrived, before
you grew up and resorted to picking up antiques and
opportunity off the street, always scanning for the next.

Inevitably, the lesson turns up as you ask, if not the
castle and not the inn and not the forest, *where? Where?
Where?* You ask the sky, ask the lover, ask the innkeeper.

Sitting at a corner table by a lantern in love's glow, or in the glory of the same old battles? Until the edges of those past lives fade and you are just as you are, so listen: *there is no such thing as arrival.* There is chance, there is rest, get used to people coming and going.

Beginning

When you are born,

that is a homeland.
When you take your first steps,

that is a homeland.
When the smoke clogs your young lungs,

when you leave with no idea of return,
that is still a homeland.

Ghazal: Storyboard

somewhere a painter and a poet of a thousand and one stories—
their divorce broke like a wave, became a news story.

after, a sick girl–though now a woman–fled to one woundful home. six months into recovery
a friend sneaks her number to the waiter. the daughter of a painter and a poet is no love story.

two years before recovery, a wildness in the air: jackets worn, shoes a father
will insist on polishing, friends holding gloved hands, this, her adventure story.

two years into recovery the landlady says, *it's just across the noodle place,*
you'll know where it is. there, sick girl meets her on the second story.

says the sick girl to lover: do not break apart my mosaic will to leave. though rosy-cheeked,
it's unhealthy. *here* is just so i can look back and say, *oh yes, a small part of my story.*

somewhere, the landscape black, universe full of stars, some make out constellations of the Nile,
or the lights of Los Angeles. in any case, there's a poet, a painter, and this is an immigrant story.

the landlady says, *it's my tiniest studio.* when sick girl moves in the window shakes
from the street's music, it seems to say, *My Hope, this is your story.*

Old Apartment/Old Language

I
In the old apartment,
the stairs were wide like a castle's
and the ceiling tall like heaven,
but everything seems bigger
reflecting back, the nostalgia mixing
with child's memory like a recipe
for enlarging something,
and if you drink it up too much
this is how you come to create dwellings in your mind
creating spaces bigger than what is deserved,
thoughts clouding more landscape than what is right,
this my first kingdom.

II
In my old language, we have many words
for love. The professor makes a diagram,
love as it relates to beauty, your breath, your hawa,
and we follow the diagram arrow upwards
(for intensity) where it
becomes loves of longing–*showq*[1]–
here I learn that this word for love sounds like
the word for thorns–*showk*[2]–
but *showq* is a deeper sound at the end than *showk*,
perhaps longing cuts deeper than thorns.
Even when I climb to the top of the steps of the old Cairene apartment,
look at the streets below,
I drink up lessons on how to become a woman,
watching from a distance from a window.

One day, I learn to long for the old.
One day, the longing grows too big.

---

1   شوق
2   شوك

6

The First Kingdom/Quartier Populaire

—inspired by Quartier Populaire by Zeinab Abdel Hamid

You are a small child at the precipice of your Cairene apartment balcony.
Like your father's shoulders, like a tower for a princess,
it is an enchanting place to witness the below.

Right on schedule—*Bikya[1] bikya! Old junk, old junk!*
You hear the same collector yell everyday
as he strides up & down the same sunny streets.
Hand-holding your parents, you cross the video game main road,
there are thrills here but it is safe like a swinging cradle. But now
do you spot this next entrance, a pop of pink clouds
gathered on one long stick like a sorcerer & his wand—
Who wants cotton candy? Your parents unlock his magic with coins in hand,
descending into this quarter that was just once a green mound of land,
you grumpily squeezing through women's bottoms dressed in robes
& gripping your father's lifeline of a hand among wagons & baskets full of greens
& corpses of cows hanging like red-pink curtains
& the kingdom is prosperous.

Each character on the street is a friend or a sundial,
so loud here like child's play, the shuffle of shibshib[2], car engines, white noise,
like you are such a part of it that you don't know you love it
until you learn to equate love with loss.

One day the buildings rise & cover the view from your Giza balcony,
new neighbors pinched into this alleyway of a street.
Like the trash heap that was once the grazing field for the water buffalo,
the routine is changed. They make plans to cover these dust roads in cement
& a metro one day, but the kingdom bears its street names—
You learn them now to find your way.

You are now a woman in a new apartment
where too many sounds are missing here:
the clockwork orchestra lost to a car alarm here, a gunshot there.
You sweep the streets now, searching—

---

1   بكيا
2   شبشب

Bikya bikya! What remains, what remains!

Khaki

While in war in Sinai, dunes like a crumpled
handkerchief, perhaps my father wore such a shade

the color of Amman,
a city painted with a simple palette,

the color of skirts past fingertip length
in school to pass inspection (or not)

a far cry from gold–sometimes–if you think wishfully, mix your paints too muddily
not a far cry from the color of my skin after I stopped being called *brownberry*

not a far cry from crying on the sidewalk's same sandy tone,
from Halloween lions, wicker chairs, and baskets,
stained carpeting of my mother's house—

caresses the countless rugs she's layered from the dusty streets of Tersa and Al Zorayqy,
border of a patchwork quilt built of carpets,
same shade as the imaginary border of a desert.

Foundation

My mother said she left my father
in the first city
to find she had to return to him.
This measure of love
is to quantify it
by way of leaving it behind.
The measure of his love
was what remained of it
when she returned.
These are the lessons I was taught,
that love must be fragmented,
return must be a question,
and home is never where you think.

Sami's Fairytale

The last fairytale is when you return
and your aunt's lipstick stains your cheek
and the homecoming is no longer a homecoming
but a welcoming to what is unfamiliar
but is, somehow, yours.
The Return is a fairytale—
just a story you made up to survive

and make it through the days you weren't at home
in a place people assign to you as
Home. Picturing it over and over again,

this story is not so convincing, the plot never quite makes it past the airport, this trapped-in-a-
tower-climbing-your-hair-out-I-am-back-movie-montage-moment
with the right song– *an Arabic song?*
a mosaic of faces, you can't quite make out everyone's features, but surely
it's your tallest cousin, your cousin with the big smile,
your cousin with the long hair and the heart that is just like yours,
the aunt who makes you laugh,

it is them,
and they are the mosaic that shows you everything, though fragmented, will fall into place.
When you greet your family again you speak your language perfectly.
You've been studying everyday just to get back to them, back to
your old language, the one you hardly get to use anymore,
but in this fairytale it is yours more than just like the old letters from boys
that collect dust in your jewelry box.
It is yours in the way that true-love-conquers-all-fairytale-
always-around-and-never-leave-you-alone-i-promise-i'll-call-you-back-and-he-does
kind of way.
The unquestionable way, like how others view
Home.
You avoid that word—
I am going to my *house*,
I am going to my *father*,
I am going to my *mother*,
the way some people avoid fairytales—

boring-cliche-so-you-think-about-everything-faraway-okay.
At least you have a house, a father, and a mother.
That is the beginning of this story that is not a fairytale
but it is yours.

Necklace Fairytale

The magician's assistant ran away
after she bought a chain so small
she could wear gold or silver earrings
and no one would notice the mismatch.
She bought one so small and delicate
that only the closest people,
the ones who lean forward close enough
or whose eyes linger on her skin
can see what it is.

She buys a cloak to travel across continents
like a silhouette dressed in shadow.
She can hardly be seen as it is,
and this way she can never be found,
the audience left guessing at the glints of her eyes
as she laughs at her trick,
Was that the city lamps or the stars? Was that a flag or her dress?
They don't know where her fascination with hiding comes from,
wanting only people who squint to see her details—
she might have learned it from her parents.

First Loves

i.
Like hardened bread
I crumble at your lips.

ii.
When I left my kingdom,
my soul was disassembled
like a fallen autumn leaf
from its tree
but when I saw you
I thought you were a forest in spring.

iii.
I have two names;
everyone says the simpler one except for him.
He knows just how to pronounce it correctly
even then, it rolls so easily off his tongue
like spit.
He loves with the same
disengagement,
smooth and lazy.

I have two homes:
leaving weighs heavy
yet settles on my shoulders,
like snow.
He leaves first,
forgets I once speckled his life.
Slowly, we melt away from each other.

iv.
Rebuilding my garden wall,
filling the hole we spoke through.

Bushra

Your daddy's going to hell for not fasting, she hisses, the inference is,
so am I. I, in conversation with my camp instructor, am sixteen. Sixteen
candles of sin to burn in, I wake up every morning and see her coiffured
hair like cumulus clouds, her face first thing. Thing is, during naptime in
the cabin, she has me read Arabic passages out loud. *Loud*, she says, *recite*,
and she corrects my pronunciation, folds the words to and fro, twists them
and slaps them back in line like laundry. Laundry time: *Again*. Again and
again, so too, it becomes my favorite part of the day. Day by day, I watch
her praying while I'm bunking. Bunking together, for once foregoing lessons
for storytelling, my treasured memory of her I wasn't there for: back home,
Egypt, thirty years ago, her father approaching the front door, her and her
sisters frantically fanning the smoke out of their villa, hands butterflying
at those old wooden windows that fold in and out like accordions, having
just perched on their ledges to draw on eyebrows and lipstick in between
puffs before footsteps sounded, I imagine their speedy recovery in their
billowing floral '70s dresses, cigarettes choked and chucked out, secrets
grasped tight and to the grave, or to some sixteen year old in Minnesota
going to hell. Hell, might as well. Well, my favorite memory of me, Egypt,
seven years ago, balcony smoke from my father's cigarettes, the honeybees
in the enormous clay pot my mother claimed from the street where from it
emerged their nest, circling him and his newspaper, him telling me, *come,
sit, it will be alright*, before I knew anything of hurt or of hell. Hell, my
mother stumbled onto this vessel that was somebody's home, I stumble into
Arabic camp and come upon Bushra. Bushra; I miss her. Her, and also him.

The Carpenter & the Mermaid

"Caution and patience are no chains for a lover already chained a thousand-fold
by the tresses of his beloved."
        –from *Layla and Majnun* by Nizami Ganjavi

One day he was building a boat
at the edge of the sea
spied her peering from the water
and for many days thereafter
they loved from afar
until
driven mad with longing
he chopped down every tree
in the world
and sculpted
her image
each one finer than the next
'til at last, he captured her
in the last tree
which stole
his last breath

Portrait

speaks to your shadow, forgets you
under the stars, cuts the wood but never lights
the fire, looks like a homeland, an island,

you're just a paper boat bobbing in his sea
blue pocket, your body feeling
like an ancient remnant of your past and he circles

you, a lonely museum, paints you with
one color, one brush, photographs you but never quite pictures
things the same as you, says you speak

in waves, like you can't quite decide on which language,
wants to blow smoke in your face.

Creating waterfalls

with a limp drunken hand
that cannot bear the weight of giving water to lips
this is the first betrayal of the night
set the cup of water down like a judge who makes a sentence
on the bedside table, clang
this is the rest of your night, it says:
mouth talking with lips unkissed,
stories of not being ready and not
having the desire that often comes in bed
with someone you may even be fond of
but not ready is not ready
this was the beginning of the night, you remember:
a kiss is fine but once they leave the club, the taxi
there's no point in courting anymore
this is not jane austen
not amman
not doha
this is not
where you thought

you may be by now

just in a body
at another body's disposal
legs hanging limp
eyelids dropping like broken elevators
while all the roads from all of the maps of every place that ever raised you
seep out of your body like blood
mouth open, lips move, tongue works
and first line of defense finally successful
alright, alright, is the surrender
finally, finally eyelids given permission to close shut when the night is safe again
to fall asleep in lustful arms
this is the end of the night, day brings:
creating waterfalls
heart and body to travel along them
crushed at the bottom

for the body's betrayal from birth—
and surely something will break once it hits
but telling yourself, *i would do it all over again if i could*
go back and make it a love story
i don't feel any different
anyway

How to Exist in Three Places At Once:

Call your father.
Go to work, eat three meals in one, cry in bed.
Begin job applications.

Listen to a song in your first language.
Wake up.
Go to work.
Call your mother.

Being a Destination

I had a friend with hair that fell
in brown rivulets,
who wore makeup even when
we said we'd go to brunch
rolling out of bed,
in that time in our lives
when we had nowhere else to go because
the coffeeshop was the bedroom was the club
was the church was the tip jar
was the park grass and the sweaters spread on the grass
as makeshift blankets,

back when everything was makeshift,
the people, the friendships, and the city—
roaming in the cobblestone alleyways,
boarding the bus to a city three hours away,
throwing money at mango lassis
and into the cups of every person seated on the bridge
I worried about late at night,
waiting in line for takeout where the servers knew my name,
recognize me from recognizing our shared unbelonging,
hobbling along that cobblestone,
singing *baby, baby, baby* with a friend on the shopping streets,
curating playlists to scream along to on the walk home,
thinking, *I would love to work in a bookstore with a red door*
thinking, *I will never go back*
thinking, *this cake is the best I've ever had*
at brunch with my friend, and getting swept away under the copper
twinkling eyes of statues, kaleidoscope-stained glass buildings,
beer and sky and stars, bouncing onyx and chocolate off each other,
glistening 'til the day overtook them and cafes set up their signs
for brunch.

Author's Note

This poem borrows a phrase from "The Huguenot Graveyard at the Heart of the City" by
Eavan Boland: "There is flattery in being a destination."

Make You a Myth

I still hope
like the myths,
that you cycle in with the seasons,
the harvest,
the proverbs that people tell themselves day by day

to be a myth is to live without touch
to love without fruition
to pay without knowing the cost.

If you cannot be here
I will make you that myth.

Flower Shopping with Frida

"I paint flowers so they will not die."
–Frida Kahlo

A parking lot corner,
beachy air, a few gourds and prices marked for "annuals"
flowers that just die by the end of the year
i wonder if Frida had annuals and knew to call them "annuals"
or if annuals inspired her to paint them *because* they always die

We aren't really shopping together
it's just me recognizing her
portrait by the cash register

What the hell is it doing in this small town market
pale faces everywhere like daisies
or ghosts
i wouldn't dare approach her, all
smock and big earrings and tied up hair and perhaps a bag strap across her body

i've met heroes before, put a foot in my mouth
and kicked myself
waiting for the right time to message remember me
so we can celeb and collaborate?
Like how my man and i keep each other at arm's length,
It's just not the right time,
i'm not who i yet want to be
in this frozen summer

Two weeks before in the same neighborhood
i walked down the street
and a man screamed
for me to go back to where i came from
three times and i wonder
if i should have thrown something at his car

take a petal out of Frida's book
paint flowers and feminism and Egyptianism
and elephants and doves

here i am instead
returning for fruit and flowers
from a distance this time

***

Maryland is nasty humid
my first fern still died a few weeks ago
ferns are *not* annuals

i'm trying to take photos more because
i can feel it all slip away
and that's something i got from Frida

Her Baba was German
i tell my Baba in Cairo on the phone
because he has the utmost respect for her
(he was called a communist freak too)
and he says
Can that be true? She's the face of Mexico
i want to ask him if people cut in half
can't be the face of anything

After the call i look out the window
and the town stares back
blue and conniving
impossible to stay,
difficult to leave,
horrible occurrences can hold a person hostage

***

Eventually the tourists flow through the market line
just passing through this place
i approach Frida and the counter with a few gourds and onions

i didn't grab any flowers
one day i too will pass it by
When i go home
i'll paint my flowers there
and bury them where they were born

cities: skyline stencil

cites with blue eyelashes,
cities with trails of music in every corner,
cities with streets like video games.

anywhere-but-here-don't-care-where cities,
let-me-in-and-i'll-give-it-all-i've-got cities,
everyone-should-get-to-see-this cities,
marry-for-a-visa cities,
built-by-the-ones-they-now-want-to-kick-out cities,
stumbled-into-one-of-my-storybooks cities,
no-one-lives-here-but-it's-still-alive cities,
be-quiet-and-eat-your-alligator cities,
get-lost-and-find-an-unmapped-bakery-with-the-world's-best-brownies cities,
left-my-home-had-no-choice-but-to-leave-only-asking-that-you-want-me-back
cities.

cities with people layered like cake,
cities with narrow alleys, flavored smoke,
orange trees like freckles on a face.

Out of the Palace: Helen of Troy

You once held my feet in your lap and said
you drank away enough of your edges,
that we'd fit just right,
speak to each other in ways that
can't properly translate to other languages,
and the map I used must be blessed
because how else could I
wind up here and be
with you?

It's different when I'm here alone,
the language not mine.
This whole kingdom wants someone unlike me to be yours,
uses insults that I wear like dresses—
there are worse ways to go about losing things,
a shoe lost on a stair becomes a fairytale.
Thought I'd be royalty but this feels more like I'm
a lady-always-in-waiting
always in transit.

I'm not serving right anymore,
can't serve you or me or them or the ones outside these borders,
did everything I could to stay,
tore apart then unburied every reason, wrote the love letters,
made my declarations 'til people could excuse me for what I was—
I thought I was a romantic and I would have waited
but so long in stillness and you become your own mirage
when the light seems clearest
until you don't have any more certainty.

And I want to go home—
I know that place doesn't exist but if it did
it's definitely not here.
And that's the sweetest drink I've had
since downing nectar, playing with fate.

My heart will take a few months to catch up to my decision, my head,
my body,
it always does—
tells anyone that will listen, myths: *You belonged there for a bit.*
I still think they think about you.
You were so happy for a bit.
Bit by bit it will get easier.
I think you'll stop this leaving and it will stop happening to you.

Yasmine's Fairytale

Baba said, *I lived through a war and that's something not many people have done.*
Look at you, how many young girls your age have been able to do these things,
look at your passport,
when the security guard says it's heavy, I tell them you travel a lot, full of visas we can't have,
separate you from me to be proud of you,
I think that's why I must have put you on another continent in the first place.

He went to war, you fall asleep trying to imagine,
wake up the next day,
go to work at another coffeeshop, wonder when you will see Baba again,
know you will never see that screaming guy again,
but the stupid–and loving–part of you asks for return.
Him, time, your father, the first country, the old life, the old coffeeshop–
all of it.

When I Grow Up

When I grow up,
I want to be a child again.

I will pierce my skin
for every metaphorical hole in my chest
for every key of every place
I've loved and given away.
I will have so much metal inside–hoops, studs, chains—
that no man will dare say
I'm not a treasure.
When they bury me, they'll say,
here lies the queen in her jewels,
she never shared them with anyone.

For every citizen who tells me I'm a sheep or a terror,
I'll never be their diplomat or their bridge.

When I grow up,
I will save the cheetahs and join the swim team.
I'll never leave, or if I do, it'll be just to say
I have a place to come back to.
A message in a bottle that stays the same:
preserved like my culture.

When I grow up,
I'll go back to Muscat

and raise hell,
I'll go back to Amman

and be courted properly.
When I grow up, I'll always remember to call Patricia and Aisha.

I'll flee for fun but I'll never be told where to go
and I'll never come when beckoned.
I'll fall asleep every night surrounded by noisy streets and a silent mind.
I won't mythologize my life,

I'll legalize being too softhearted.
I'll never be asked *why did you stay*, instead, *how did you leave so fast?*
I leave because I'm good at it.

When I grow up, I'll age like a country.
You'll remember me for who I was supposed to be
and not who I became.

Smith Island Cake Fairytale

Craft me a potion,
pour your finest ingredients,
pay for my coffee with no intention
of taking anything in return,
pick me blooms of baby's breath behind my back
and surprise me with a sheepish smile
all over again.
I would bake ten layers of batter thin as ice
and spread silky fudge on every crevice
to sustain you
in a boat white and wooden
on the lone waters
and wait until your return,
craft each of my messages to you
and wait for your reply,
wondering if anything I send you
holds meaning
out in the world
when you're away from mine—
wondering
if you think of me in this distance
like you would
with each bite of cake.

Surrealist Portrait: An Ode

A dangerous tongue makes bridges
where they never should have burned,
where they shouldn't have been built.
Distance doesn't exist
if you make a laugh of a canyon,
a toss of an ocean,
an ignorance from a flattery.
You only see
the oasis in a desert
so really, you don't see anything.

You think paths are something to trace
along someone's back
and borders are an invitation.
You have the attitude of someone who believes in miracles
even when you ride the tube home and it takes too long.

The fortune tellers beg to answer you
when it's not your right to even know.
You don't even mean it when you leave Trojan horses
in the wrong hearts.
You turn up when a pessimist is drinking
coffee on the hilltop
saying to themselves
every-day-here-tastes-like-smoke-every-man-here-tastes-like-ash
and just like that,
some kind of quenching is found.

You make a hurricane want to pause when you ask for things to stay the same.
You make a traveler like Ibn Batutta stop and write a postcard,
you make city statues blush
when they overhear you when you make proclamations
to your one-woman audience on the bench.
You have a charm in how you plant seeds just to wake to a forest,
a sorcery in how you turn a weekend into a lifelong journey.
You make shy things bold and bold things turn to dust.

Penelope's Lost Postcard II

If rivulets
and brooks babble and speak
as they travel home to the ocean
it's because they keep in touch.

Listen:
Do you hear it?
It's the voice of all the people I left behind
and the ones who willingly left me,
or perhaps it's destiny's whisper on the wind
saying, *you will always be this way*—
leaving or left.

I look to the stars, and like you,
they are cocky creatures,
cloaked and invisible during the day,
appearing by night,
the worst kind of lovers,
two-faced and out of reach,
the best kind of gods,
long dead and still shining.

Listen:
I'm a continent older

than I used to be and soon there will be no sea,
only land,

lined and dry like lingerie on a clothesline—
everyone will see me and feel slightly intrigued and ashamed.

We look for a place where identity will not feel negotiated,
and sometimes the last one we think of is our country.

Keep in touch while you travel home,
out of reach like a star.

Postcard from Nowhere

Fact: The sculptor who knits, paints jewelry and moonlights
as a barista, of course speaks in both body and poetry,
      asked me to marry him with a cheap bracelet in hand
      and a promise to princess me every car ride.
No, it wasn't a bracelet, it was a leatherbound copy of Yeat's *Irish Fairy Tales*
and the promise was to divorce in five years
so I could stay in Dublin longer.
It was more of an "arrangement," this being my last night there—
      Actually we were in Miami
on the beach, laying side by side in the sand
whispering the most ridiculous things:
What if my hands felt like rubber gloves,
would you still love me?
Why don't you marry me?
      Actually we were in Nashville
where he introduced me to his friend John
and said I was the poet and that's when I knew he loved me—
      No, no, wrong person, wrong fantasy—
The sculptor in Dublin handed me this paperback
said an "asshole" wrote it and he didn't want it
and *I* said yes to marrying him. He seemed nice and
I had nowhere else to go.
(Well I had two places to go but I just *couldn't* go, shall I explain the
          difference?)
We both lived in the seventh district, didn't know it, and he caught me
      grocery shopping once.
Another time I got off the bus and he sped by on his bike before he saw me
      and spun back around,
and if that's not a romantic beginning, a romantic coincidence, I don't know
what is,
    he said, *I've been wanting to hang out with you loads.*
We forged text messages together to tell the authorities– sorry, the neighbors–we
were in love and our marriage was true. We got so good at it,
living in an apartment,
      lying and thieving,
that we thought we'd make more crimes together—
that's when we robbed the bank,

hid on rooftops,
camped in West Cork–actually, Chefchaouen, where I'm writing to you now—

Actually, I never said yes to him and that's my problem;
Actually, it wasn't the sculptor at all.
The other barista, who the sculptor said hated women, also noticed me.
He gave me free cups of coffee, and flattering texts
and a child—
just kidding, I was the child but I didn't know it and I didn't know him,
But *the sculptor* sounds better than
the barista the sculptor-barista accused of hating women,
even if I lost him at the end, well,
he lost me,
more so he purposely did,
                              like a coin into a river,
                              the plop when it sinks,
and I know you're going to ask, *so did he really hate women?*
What if I told you I was the sculptor-barista,
and I just knew my coworker hated women
and took making coffee
too seriously?
Or what if I told you he loved women and he proposed and it just didn't work
out?
Or what if I told you I wasn't even worth his time that he just used the child in
me and left?
That I'm writing to you from a clinic,
a mental hospital,
no, my childhood bedroom.
That I'm deeply ashamed of who I am
and who I've become?

It's not the story you were looking for, of going
away and having a romantic adventure, is it? If only we could return
to the feeling of good stories before we knew the price.

Alright.
The woman and the child,
that was me,
and the man who called me a poet to his friend who wasn't named John
lived in Washington DC,

when I was going nowhere really at all,
and the desire said,
for once, moving, twirling girl,
Stay.
And for once that was almost alright with me,
to no longer take on disastrous beauties.

So, Strangeness, Foreignness, Homesickness: do I enliven you in every place?
Like a sibling attached at my hip, related in our faces,
I glance out into the backyard and you're dancing around naked again.

Polaroid Photo Reel

1. The Carrick-a-Rede rope bridge cliff where television kings were known to fall.
2. The same cliff face, another angle, overexposed.
3. The photo of Stoneybatter from my window, overexposed.
4. Us on the streets before we kissed goodbye outside the pub where I drew his portrait. Puppy love, girl overexposed.
5. Greek restaurant selfie, all blush, cheeks, and teeth, packed in an envelope with American chocolate and postcards.
6. My cousin and me at Khan Al Khalili, smiles and winter coats.
7. My cousin and me at the pyramids on her birthday, Giza girls in dusty shoes.
8. My parents sitting on the balcony almost exactly a year later, divorced and delightful, all deep conversation on intellectual somethings from the '70s I'll never know about.
9. My cousin eating pumpkin pie for the first time, days before her next birthday. She'd only ever seen it in the movies.
10. Us on the footsteps of the National Gallery of Art in Washington DC, where you blushed when I said I brought the camera.

Palace Garden

The question of flowers:
if you have the same seed, different soil,
how will they grow? Is one more beautiful than the other?

Hindsight is made of roses.
You will pick them apart
assuring yourself of who could have loved you.

The garlic is because I keep staying bitter
when I keep getting bit.
Gentleness is a pomegranate

pried open then collapsing into pieces,
red as wanting.
You won't find any here.

This castle surrounded by honeysuckle
exists outside of language.
All alone, I stay right here.

Faraway Mind

CONFESSION: i made a mistake.

OBSESSION: do my words bleed badness, is my being a sin? do i believe the sinister
whispers?

COMPULSION: i will flee to the countryside, dark and beckoning, find a cottage,
and live like i don't live at all, disappear like the hair from my shoulders,
my mind given all the landscape in the fields to roam.
different parts of me exist in different places,
my mind always running away to some region

of the body or soul, restless feet, losing sleep,
murmuring in my ears, flirtations from fact,
the chase from one bad thought to the next
all while standing still.

APPOINTMENT: insurance form, birthdate, birth month
two pairs and a remainder
where do i find it
on a plateau of a dune   —
on the edges of a straight branch, |
on the curve of a wave   _)
where do i give it a home
where do i give
where is the home

Garden Wall Response
after "Childhood Wall" by Ahmed Taha

You had an identity
Only when you could wear short pants on boyish legs
Pass by men in uniforms that change from black to white
Like the flick-flick-flickering of a burning match

You would have had an identity
If you named each of your street's dogs while you walked
And smelled cigarettes from a rosy balcony
Like a daily perfume

One day you say your identity is just past the corner,
The next year you say it's distance and naivety.
You're an artist in the way you can paint that innocence on a stick,
But would you wave it as your flag?

Every winter,
Would you choose to be the unborn seed over a wilted rose?

Giza

In Giza,
the boys on the rooftops,
brown and orange of dull brick,
waved their red and blue flags
and the pigeons they called home circled overtop—
it must have taken ages
the way they slowly descended.
My cousin and I watched how
home is never a direct flight
even if you have wings.

graduation

i rent a room as a studio to paint alone
i rent a room to paint away from the sounds of pots, banging doors, and familiar strangers
i rent a room to hang my flags, read the childhood posters of maps and borders i forgot about
i rent a room to pay the bills without distraction
i rent a room to spend all day with you without judgment
i rent a room to have hidden on the night i had no choice but to be taken
i rent a room to keep the things i'm still hoping to find a way to recycle someday
i rent a room to record the voices of people who deserve to be heard
i rent a room to learn to be alone without depression
i rent a room to cage my phone
i rent a room across the street from my old home, check on the cacti outside my window
i rent a room to go to when i can't stop thinking about my homes
i rent a room to be found in when i am gone too long
i rent a room to lay my head down in Bethlehem of Pennsylvania and Palestine and
Alexandria of Virginia and Egypt
i rent a room on the steps of every museum i've ever been to
i rent a room in Boston and Al Bostan to welcome old ghosts
i rent a room to house all of the memories and every journal i have for my own personal library
i rent a room in front of that room so no one will find it, much like a maze
i rent a room for when the coffeeshop gets too expensive and i can't stand to stay in my house so
i rent a room with an armchair and coffee and a mantle
i rent a room in my mother's house that is not my old childhood bedroom for a restful sleep away
i rent a room on my father's balcony
i rent a room to hide the old beer bottles kept on the balcony
i rent a room where even the landlord can be rented out
i rent a room to keep all that is important

one by one
i rent the whole world

The Carpentress & the Merman

Curled up in a surf shack
More sand than couch, he says.
We rinse off our limbs and wrap them together
Hoping we can tie a bow from it all,
That indeterminate sadness of loving a
Stranger or someone faraway
Or someone all wrong, coated in flaw,
Making me slimy like seaweed, but
This time it doesn't kill me.
So the waves carry merfolk in their dance
While I am a rigid thing. He brings me forth in salt
And song and summer sunset glow,
These island days are something
So let me flow once more,
Like in the days of my youth,
Before the adults put the hammer in my hand,
Pinned a nail in my foot,
Stake in my throat.
I could get used to being
Somewhere outside my life,
Somewhere outside my head,
With a man with August in his arms,
My friends and their siren song
Luring me back for a laugh, say my name,
Remind me I'm not wooden,
I can jump off a cliff and still drown.

The Local

I love a local,
baseball cap backwards
gesturing Manhattan directions
from the counter of the cafe—
blessed city life. While I grasp at my suitcase,
I love a local,
sit at the apartment with no one to call,
I love a local.
I loved what I loved and that was pretending
with The Local,
because I wished I was like
The Local, together,

we ate dinner down the street at a place everyone called
The Local.

I wanted to be a
hang-up-frames-and-nail-up-those-prints-here-to-stay local,
a hear-my-voice-and-know-which-region-I'm-from local.
I love a local who has family reunions in the DMV,
bless The Local who told me to find *a city, any city, just choose girl, choose,*
who said, *Detroit is always here for you,* local.
Best-friends-with-my-cousins-go-on-beach-trips local.
Staring at the rainbow Millenium Bridge saying, I-can't-pretend-I-understand-
what-you're-going-through local.
So wrapped up in my own head, I forget the map and I'm
no longer local.
Intentions so misplaced, not local.

Little-Italy-Little-Egypt-Little-Jamaica-little-world-little-me-
little-you-all-right-here-not-spread-like-butter.
Tell me the culture we build can never be forgotten.
That these new ribbons that tie us will transform into roots.
That I won't forget my roots. The sand, dust, and water will coat us for generations,
smooth us over and someday they'll see our fossils and say,
look, the locals.

Fool's Fairytale

Pass out their names
like they know who they are and what they possess
like they can spell that name in all kinds of languages.
Wiser ones keep it in a pocket and never utter it aloud.

Fools and their young naivete
keep every chest open full of treasure, full of heart
like a morning glowing through windows so inviting
and nighttime in shiny sidewalks from glittering puddles
from drizzled rain in Dublin.

We wear threads of the different places that bore us,
and the different places we've found ourselves together—
from Cairo to Raleigh—
and we promise each other days in New Orleans and Beirut,
but do you think we've ever looked better than
when we're at home, faces aglow from a screen
in plaid pajama bottoms, beside a nightstand with
ice cream bowls, when makeup slides off our faces
in the night and hair falls around our shoulders
like water encompassing a continent
and when I decided I will not make myself an island anymore
at the risk of being a fool?

Summer Nights Triptych

First Country
Leave the windows open,
turn the fans on,
balcony door a-flutter.
The night air sleeps beside you
just as the sheets do,
sweat accepted under both the stars
and sun here. Wake up
to a prayer remembering
how hard it was to fall asleep in the heat.

Second Country
Turn on the AC,
you can afford it this season.
Wrap yourself in blankets, how you like it,
turn on the fan pointed at you, keep shutters
and windows down lest the neighbors see
you, awaken in a cocoon in the dead of summer,
a body in a coffin just how it likes it.

My Country
I loved you in summer, I waited for you in winter,
Lena's mom Rania spins me around,
Bemidji, Minnesota, all of us in line to shower
gesticulating in dramatics,
singing Fairouz with the back of her hand to forehead,
me, twelve years old, feigning embarrassment.
I loved you in summer, I waited for you in winter.

We all lost touch by spring.

Love Language

The merchant would read to the neighbor's daughter,
the lively one who could neither read nor write.
They married one day. Bore children.
Their second son was cleverest in his class at memorizing the Qur'an
than the teacher himself. He read books aloud to his father
most nights, Baba's hands folded behind his cushioned head,
mustache reflecting lightbulb, this their language of love.
This second son would become a writer.
Meet a woman who could read and write in two languages:
his and hers. Baba died before meeting his grandchildren.
The second son's second daughter reads brokenly aloud to him.

A new language of love must be created.
An old language of grief is reciprocated.

Palace Sunset

There was and there was not
a beggar who remembered and forgot her days
as sultan all at once,
so much so she became sick.
What is it to not always want

to return
to something that you should have,
would have had, if not for a twist of fate?
And maybe still *could* have,
but not how you wanted.

Tell the beggar there's a sultan in the palace
with an uncanny resemblance. The beggar stared at the ocean
and moon like any traveler, sometimes thought
she saw her family in the grocery store,
that the bus driver had her father's silhouette

'til he turned around.
Nothing more heart-wrenching

than seeing the other side of the palace
and feeling you don't belong,
or that you *do*, beggar-sultan says.
You can just taste what you desire
but can't quite stomach it.

That sultan who taunted the beggar,
that dream that tricked the world,
loss that turns to madness when
you could have imagined life without it,
while someone else rules this kingdom,

someone's got to tell it,
it's everyone's fate
to watch from below the palace window and wish
they had it, see, the palace always changes

and you're one of the lucky ones who will sedate it.

The beggar is always lost, not what she's looking for,
she uses the wrong tools, she needs a mirror, only.
One day she wakes up again. First the sickness comes,
and a new beauty must be found upon awakening,
even if it's the palace's dusk,

the falling of a dream.

A Dream

On the shores of sleep in another world,
I saw your face for the first time

in nearly a year,
in some part of the universe, maybe outer space,

black sky, white stars, our faces dimmed in lavender light,
shining like crystals–or simply

a world unlike ours,
living in the grey.

The first I dreamt of you where what remained
was only wistful peace in our minds—

maybe they really did greet each other
somewhere in the stars

on ships entering ports of hypnotic shores.
I like the idea of us saluting from across a harbor,

pirates on our ships, secret knowledge on each other's sins.

Always Loves

We silently agree to keep driving in circles
around this smallest of towns
just to make something of the night.
The highways, the rich neighborhoods along the water
where they called us trespassers.
Let's go to New York,
you suggest when we pass the green sign,
not sure if you are joking
because we always want to leave—

we drive around and shuffle songs,
become fortune tellers, muses,
whisper questions into the phone and pray
the next lyric becomes an answer.
We created something of a hovel and home
in a bland apartment with a smell of paint.
Fanned the smoke of the wrong pan
and nailed together the frames—
made something of the empty and tell each other on the phone,
you can have everything you've ever wanted
even if it's different from what you imagined—

the always loves, the ones who meet you in DC,
who keep other people's promises because someone had to,
who ride the planes and if they can't afford the ticket
or get the visa, they send you the voice notes in your first language—

Even when I can't give you every sonnet,
every word of my language,
every moment of time we lost together
in all the distance—

I give you all my love
and my thanks.

Last Love: Amoula's Fairytale

Amoula,
    you were born a pessimist

maybe even a mistake

your father naming you after lonely women
who could write words that shone like cities,

and your mother

a whole other spelling meaning, "my hope."

They said you'd become a woman
    but you became a statue.

Amoula,
    you look at everything like a prophecy

especially when you're nowhere
near the pharmacy with the meds and the gummies,
all the doctors' offices

where you've said, *I'm ready, take whatever it is,*
I'll submit,
    swallow constellations star by star
                'til I've enough light within me to be a god
because you never wanted to be anything less.

Goddess, the schoolchildren once jeered
to a walking good-bye in baggy trousers.

Amoula,
your best friend's mom said no one
can be taken seriously if their names end with "y."
    Your Hope
can't be taken seriously
and neither can lonely women who crowd words
to make cities

They said you'd become a dancer
and when you look up and squint
you don't see it,
you don't even see a face in the mirror.

Amoula,
just open the love letter like you haven't been bitten thrice.
Open the front door like you can see friends past the glass,
like you take Hope seriously.
Open your borders, just try.

Objects

The old wife
suspected it was one of her husband's jokes
that he got his daughter to buy her the long skirt

so she threw it in the closet.

Their son, embarrassed, had been given an oud
by his grandfather, who recounted his sweet days in Shobra
and Chicago

so he threw it in the closet.

Their daughter stole her father's cigarettes
after witnessing another of his coughing fits,
but knew he checked the trash,

so she hid them in the closet.

All of the leftover objects collected in a mass
that walked in a skirt, floated on smoke
and hummed with an oud's music in the haze.

It plucked and placed teardrops on grass leaves for the morning
made shadows through windows in the evening
and locked the door again after itself
before settling back inside, strewn on the closet floor
so even when they would check days or years later,
each person could have their certainties.

Marilena

I bought the same pink clearance top twice
to be a belle at a ball or a club, had money

only some of the time,
nannied children with soft accents,

made coffees for older men
who tipped well. Lavender-aproned girls,

excited when one regular would come
in for his cup brandishing his

2 euro coins 'til he said he admired
our figures, round as mugs, and one day

tried to follow me home. I ducked into
a thrift shop, hid in the racks, little me

shrouded in chiffon. Scared of life,
I saw ghouls for years, ditched the pink top,

wore my bra out, drank from strangers' cups.
I remembered Marilena from that old cafe,

who had a photography exhibit in a city gallery,
left a boyfriend back home in Italy, said

he was bad news. She was 26
so I figured she knew what she was talking about,

marveled at what a "spinster" could be.
She sued the cafe that withheld our wages,

left to work downtown in an ice cream shop.
We couldn't text much for our language barrier

but sometimes I saw her ponytailed head
through the glass windows. I wish I hadn't

spent my time so wrong,
writer's block at every bakery

on the block,
let myself get paid badly under the table, misused under

the sheets. I learned "a job was a job"
desire to be chosen while Marilena learned never

to settle. When I was 26, I got out,
got help, tried to be like Marilena,

wherever she is.

Work of Art

These walls, like you, were eagerly awaiting
the arrival of something beautiful
in a neighborhood of orange and red bricks.

The fridge is lined with cards from people you love—
they are still far away—
the neighbor said hi even when you averted your gaze.

You love to stay in bed like a matchbox
while the snow ricochets outside, you used to run
at any chance and could never sit still.

You don't pretend anymore
mixing hot sauce with ketchup,
ordering two slices of cake.

You live inside a work of art:
the floorboards have cracks and filth
from a long and twisted past. Then again, so does yours.

You put putty in those cracks, colored in the floorboards,
and there are cracks in the ceiling, too, like someday
this might all cave in.

What is a heart burning from a distance?

Apology in Arabic

Sorry I used a cliché to tell you
my baggage won't fit into your boxes
or moving trucks.

I'm sorry your voice was embroidery,
and I couldn't trace it with my fingers
fast enough.

Sorry my voice is a whisper,
a snowflake collapsed
into the earth. One-of-a-kind, gone

and never remembered.

Postcard to Comparison
((& Postcard to New Love))

today, sitting outside the metro,
i wish someone would
paint me on this bench

                              ((someone can consider my
                              worst moment
of winter   beautiful,
centuries from now, people   would view my rendering,
say,   so poetic,
so tragic.

you took   my observer

to another town because
i drank from your cup,   dreamed of a girl who looked like me,
but different, better.

"comparison is   the thief
of joy,"
but they
didn't say   she could pickpocket you on the street, your bed,
she would steal your breath   without warning, a robber in the best dress,
and as   she runs away
for her crimes,
she whisks away like a spiral
of genie's smoke,   like she did you some favor.
but that's exactly what you did.

                              today,
you swindled me
outside the metro
beside a cat with a swollen lip,
beside a mother and her baby in a blanket,
and on the other side of me

                              two lovers. i laugh.
the absurdity:
every role the world assigns me laid out here—

Mother, Lover, or Alone.
somebody, anybody, else in jars,

every wish,
thinking that maybe

would tire of coming by and

i could remember

outside the metro

the cat won't even comfort me
after you stole
we both peer around
the square, after you flee.
if this was

the cat wouldn't have
a swollen lip
it would

you'll look through
see Comparison up to her
usual tricks, she will stop
skipping, say she's sprained
her ankle and

but you'll say no,
not anymore.
the cat didn't speak,
so i'm writing this to you
instead.

mother and her baby are
a friend

from the metro.
they walk

i used to store the hope of being

bottled

one day,
you
saying, i'm just here for a drink.
wishing

waiting

without your touch.

today's joy,

a fairytale

covered in dust,

say to me right now,
one day
your window,

come in, you
always say, yes, yes, of course,

directly

greeting

emerging

side by side

past the square, their coats   dancing in the wind,
keep laughing

and i   look up
the nearest post office,   remember
my own address is yours,   and then roam
the nearest art galleries
seeking   the joy))
you've been hoarding.

Off the Airplane

I never regretted the tickets or the fleeing
never looked from one start date to the next
never felt better than when I was flying

instead of watching things fly by.
Now I'm on the other side and feel serenity
in this bed, beside a best friend on the couch

with a furry creature on my lap.
Cooking breakfasts on Saturday mornings that tip toe

into afternoons so quietly we don't notice,
coffee shop days until the two hours before close.
This is so different to the happiness I knew
the old voice asking
do you have to leave to know
do you have to leave just to go
and
   did you call your father today
       and
     who do you serve if you stay

And living takes money I will say
money takes a surrender to spending on stillness,
papayas and parsley,
linen and candles,
the enemies and the losses,
not just the gains

My achilles heel: distance

is a cost
this love is a currency
don't let it   blow away

The Cottage

I'd drop my last life gliding
through my fingers like sand, wash up
on this new shore tired again
of being stuck, old waters clinging
like tea on a biscuit, but I know the sun

here could forgive, dry my dress.

Locals say the plankton will glow
at your toes, rooms are grief
with seashell decor, the smell of nature
harsh as life itself, swamps craggy
on one bank, waves debating on the other.

Here, I could awaken in gentle
white frills when day trips over
the moon spilling its cocktail,
be the linen caressing soft one,
not the mess for once, forgetting

I dreamed in denim and concrete.

After spring flowers, I could bloom, see
the convenience stores, fast food restaurants
red and yellow mosaic
of Main Street, could drop everything
right now and spy the tentacles

of the Milky Way
Don't we all move and imagine

if we stopped someplace, we never would?

I'll muddy my dress, throw on regret,
but you can't miss something

to return,
you can only miss it to death.

Leftovers & Crumbs

Looking back,
it's all just fadalat[1] and fatafet[2]
and my mother always said,
leaving food on the plate makes you look ungrateful
and don't eat on the couch where it doesn't belong
lest you leave bits on the floor—
it's all leftovers and crumbs,
throw them or eat them,
take it or leave it.

But–I chewed more
than I could swallow,
hungered too much,
chased and the distance grew larger.
I hungered for more than the slices they offered,
I wanted the whole cake and was given half,
there is only an inheritance, a future,
pieces like the first kingdom, but no king.
And a dream where finally, I do not mourn

the loss of you, the loss of them, the daydream

or the homeland.

A dream where there were no more leftovers
and no more crumbs.

---

1   فضلات
2   فتافيت

End

When you are dead,

that is return.
When you take your first steps to the square with a new lover,

that is return.
When the smoke clogs your lungs at twenty,
when you leave him with no way to reach you,

that is still, return.

There is still love in distance,
and there is still distance in love,

loss in return, relief in a leaving,
bringer of life brings death,
bringer of distance will one day bring a closeness

they didn't even have to earn.

acknowledgements

Thank you to the editors behind the publications that first gave my poems homes at *Trampoline*, *Sienna Solstice*, *Plentitudes*, *Running Dog*, *Mizna*, and *Tupelo Press*. Thank you Lana Barkawi, Naomi Riddle, and Kirsten Miles.

Trampoline Poetry (2019) published "Portrait," "graduation" and "Polaroid Photo Reel."
Sienna Solstice (2020) published "Flower Shopping with Frida."
The Plentitudes Journal published "Bushra."
Running Dog (2022/2023) published through a micro-residency "Arrival" and "Postcard to Comparison ((Postcard to New Love))."
Mizna (Winter 2023/2024) published "Ghazal: Storyboard."

Thank you to the ones who gave me a closeness I didn't even have to earn: Baba and Mama for always encouraging me to write. To Ahmed, who regularly takes me around the best bookstores in Cairo and always thought I would write a book. To Rissie, who always supported my words, for my fifth grade birthday present, *D'Aulaires Book of Greek Myths*, and for also having so many tales from *A Thousand and One Nights* in both English and Arabic. To Patricia, for giving me the gift card that I used to buy *Ella Enchanted* and didn't seem to mind that as a child I would read at every family gathering. To Aisha, whose love was unconditional and whose life I ask about like a child asks to hear a tale over and over again. To 'Amu Abduh for always asking me what book I was reading, even if it was in English. I miss you all. Thank you to Charlie, Mervet, Hayat, and Hind for many meals and stories over the years that this manuscript was written, and to Lelia, Rana, Nirvana, Mai, Hamada, Taha, and many more of my family members for carrying on the family legacy of art, and whose vigor inspires me.

Thanks to my grandfather Taha for once upon a time asking my father to read to him for a shilling, cementing the love of literature that runs in the family. To my brother, Taha, for all of the fun, all of the love, and all of the joy of being an older sibling for the first time. To my extended family who were joined through an intercultural marriage and have always accepted me, despite long periods of being away, and who welcome me back always.

Thank you to the following people who read earlier versions of my poems: Jake W., Claire K., Olivia B., Michelle K., Kiki, Keri, Elise, Hannah, Moya, Myriem, and Berlanty, who taught and inspired me and who I regret losing touch with;

To Amena, Salma, and Rachel for those talks in the kitchen of the Garden City apartment; To Ereny for the late-night identity chats; To Hala, my tutor and friend; To Jessica Abughattas for workshopping and editing with "Postcard from Nowhere," "Being a Destination," "Marilena," and "Surrealist Portrait: An Ode."

Special thanks to the creative writing faculty at University College Dublin, the very first time I received any kind of acceptance for my writing, which inspired me to begin submitting to journals and contests. To Dr. D and others who gave me years of treatment, without which I wouldn't have been able to submit a manuscript. To Mills Parole Elementary School for introducing me to the poetry of Langston Hughes, and to Professor David Moore for teaching me all about him. I haven't stopped wondering. To my professors and cohort at UM, especially Eli and Evan.

My undying gratitude goes to Fady Joudah and Haya Charara of the *Etel Adnan Poetry Prize*, for telling me years ago that this manuscript would one day become a book. Thank you for believing in my work and for the tremendous support.

Thanks to the Elyssar Press team for their dedication to the publication of this book. Thank you to Katia Hage for granting me this dream. To Allie Rigby, for the editing of these poems. Working with you was a joy. To Nicole Khoury and Amena Sharaf for the sensitivity readings. Huge thanks to Stephanie Aoun for her design skills, patience in realizing my vision, and incorporating an old painting of mine into the front cover, inspired in part by Hung Liu's *Persephone*. Thank you so much for helping to make my dream come true.

To Cairo.

author bio

Emily Ahmed is an Egyptian-American writer and artist. Her poems are published in *Trampoline*, *Sienna Solstice*, *Plentitudes*, *Running Dog*, *Mizna*, and more. She studied Arabic, Middle Eastern Studies, and art in Minnesota and throughout North Africa and Southwest Asia.

On Distance is her first book of poetry.